The Letter Ww

The Ocean

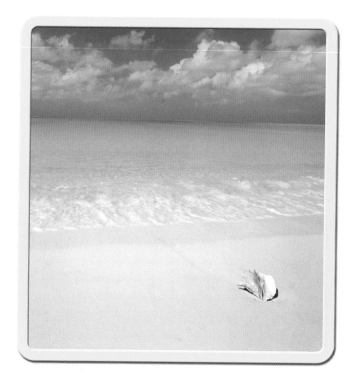

by Hollie J. Endres

I can see the **w**ater.

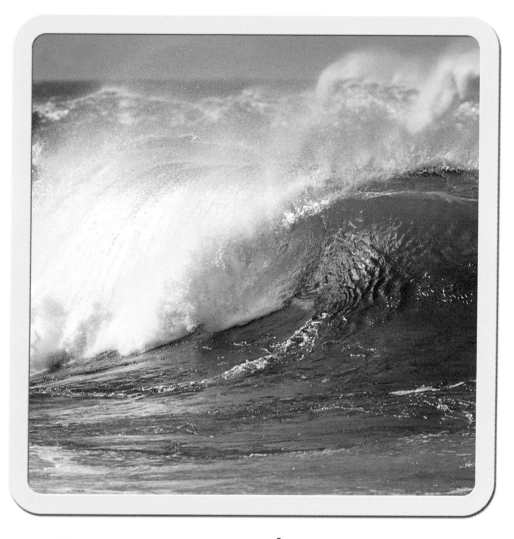

Can you see the **w**aves?

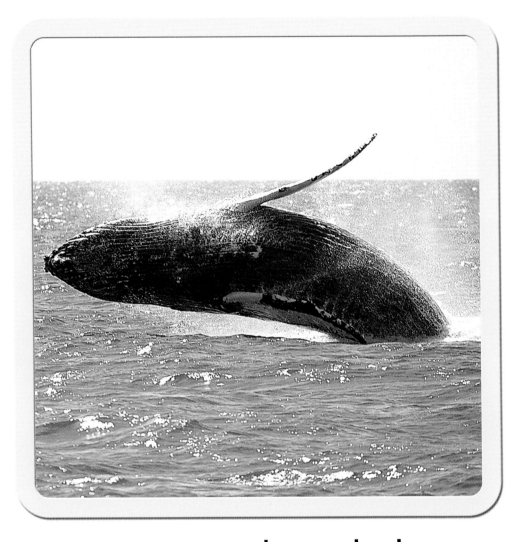

I can see the **w**hale.

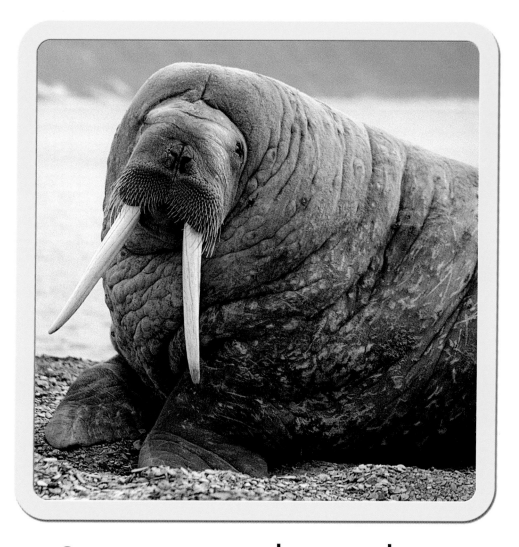

Can you see the **w**alrus?

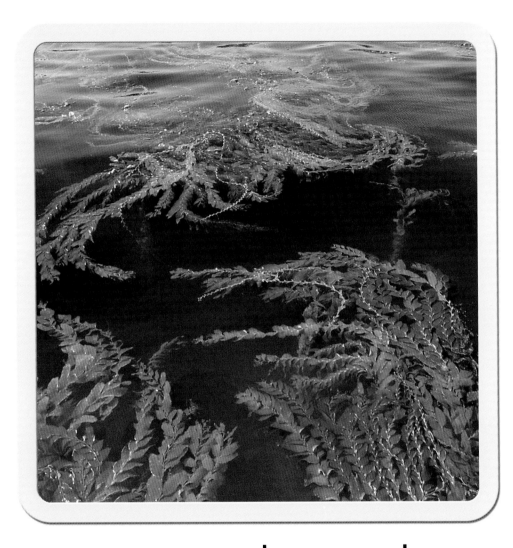

I can see the **w**eeds.

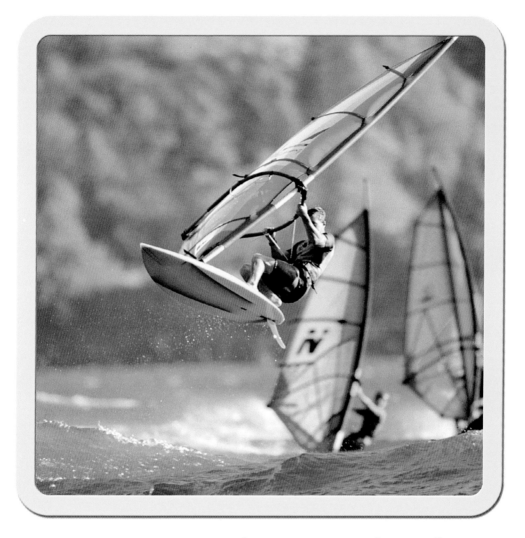

Can you see the **w**indsurfers?

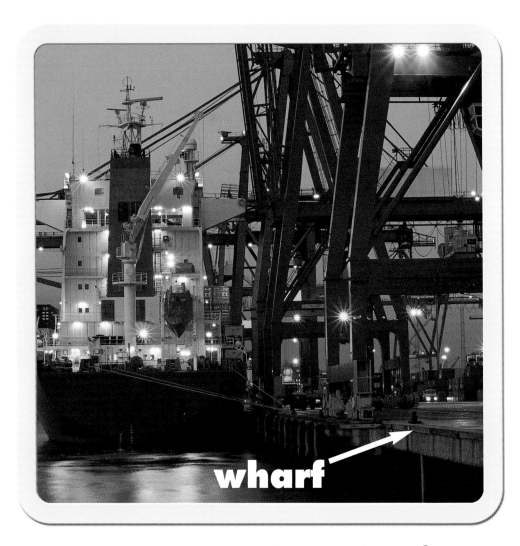

wharf

I can see the **w**harf.